The Last Cigarette

adapted from Simon Gray's
The Smoking Diaries
and other memoirs

by
SIMON GRAY
and
HUGH WHITEMORE

faber and faber

First published in 2009
by Faber and Faber Limited
74–77 Great Russell Street, London WC1B 3DA

Typeset by Country Setting, Kingsdown, Kent CT14 8ES
Printed in England by CPI Bookmarque, Croydon, Surrey

A version of the introduction was first published
in the Royal Literary Society magazine in 2008

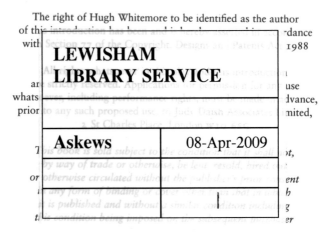

A CIP record for this book
is available from the British Library

ISBN 978-0-571-24409-6

2 4 6 8 10 9 7 5 3 1

Writing with Simon

It was a glorious evening in a glorious garden in Holland Park. There was a party. Music from a string quartet. Simon and his wife, Victoria, arrived late. He'd been to see his doctor to get the results of a medical check-up, tests and so on. 'Bad news,' he said, in a whisper (as if not to disturb the elegant jollity all around), 'it's in my lung, not much they can do about it.'

We followed them away from the party, down Kensington Place to a restaurant, where we sat winded and stunned by the news. Somehow we found something to laugh about; we always found something to laugh about.

A few weeks later, Simon rang – we rang each other most days, to gossip, to analyse the Test Match, to disparage the work of other writers. A producer had been in touch with Simon's agent (my agent too) to see if he would consider dramatising his book *The Smoking Diaries*. 'I can't do it,' he said, 'I just don't have the energy. Why don't you do it?' I was of course enormously moved that he should ask me. 'I can't,' I said. 'It wouldn't be right – but we could do it together.' Simon said he needed to think it over. By this time, Christmas was approaching. My wife and I were going to Hampshire, and I suggested that I try to write a very rough first draft over the holidays. I had the idea that the play should be a dialogue exchange between three Simon Grays (one of them a woman). Simon didn't think it would work and said so fairly forcibly. Undeterred, I scrambled together a first draft, sent it to Simon, and got a phone call almost immediately. 'You're right. It works.'

We decided to establish a routine. We would meet every afternoon in Simon's house and write until he became too tired to concentrate (usually about three hours). This seemed to work well. We were both creatures of habit. I would leave my house, by Kensington Church Street, and walk down the hill to Holland Park. We met at Lidgate's, where Simon introduced me to a hideously addictive honeycomb confection called Hokey-Pokey: bad for the weight, even worse for the teeth.

I would sit in one of the swivel chairs while Simon crouched over the computer. Neither of us had collaborated like this before, and both, I think, found it the greatest fun once we conquered our initial shyness. There's something awfully intimate about writing a play – and it was odd (to say the least) discussing Simon's approaching death as material for a stage entertainment.

> SIMON Now look – the scene where I get the news of the tumour – should that be the end of Act One or the beginning of Act Two? What do you think?

> HUGH End of Act One, surely? Terrific end to Act One.

> SIMON Good for bar trade, anyway. They'll all need a drink after that.

And so we'd laugh, Simon spluttering and reaching for another Silk Cut.

Simon lived to an idiosyncratic timetable: bed at dawn, rising at noon, which meant that when I started work at nine-ish (in the morning) there would be a sheaf of overnight emails from Simon, full of spontaneous wit and observation and penetrating self-examination. Simon wrote like a great jazz musician plays – a cascade of improvisatory riffs – rhythmic, daring, utterly unique.

When our first draft was finished, we both felt bereft. The afternoons were strangely empty. We had dinner with the producer and discussed who might direct the play. A name was mentioned. 'He's not free until November,' said the producer. 'Too late!' said Simon, exploding with laughter.

Alas, it was too late. He died, not of cancer, but an aneurysm. The joy and privilege of working with him will stay with me for the rest of my days – those February afternoons – so challenging, exhilarating and, above all, so tremendously full of life.

Hugh Whitemore
February 2009

Simon Gray

Simon Gray was born in 1936. He began his writing career with *Colmain* (1963), the first of five novels, all published by Faber. He was the author of many plays for TV and radio, also films, including the 1987 adaptation of J. L .Carr's *A Month in the Country*, and TV films including *Running Late*, *After Pilkington* (winner of the Prix Italia) and the Emmy Award-winning *Unnatural Pursuits*. He wrote more than thirty stage plays, among them *Butley* and *Otherwise Engaged* (which both received *Evening Standard* Awards for Best Play), *Close of Play*, *The Rear Column*, *Quartermaine's Terms*, *The Common Pursuit*, *Hidden Laughter*, *The Late Middle Classes* (winner of the Barclay's Best Play Award), *Japes*, *The Old Masters* (his ninth play to be directed by Harold Pinter) and *Little Nell*, which premiered at the Theatre Royal Bath in 2007, directed by Peter Hall. *Little Nell* was first broadcast on BBC Radio 4 in 2006, and *Missing Dates* in 2008. In 1991 he was made BAFTA Writer of the Year. His acclaimed works of non-fiction are *An Unnatural Pursuit*, *How's That for Telling 'Em, Fat Lady?*, *Fat Chance*, *Enter a Fox*, *The Smoking Diaries*, *The Year of the Jouncer*, *The Last Cigarette* and *Coda*. He was appointed CBE in the 2005 New Year's Honours for his services to Drama and Literature. Simon Gray died in August 2008.

Hugh Whitemore

Hugh Whitemore was born in 1936. He began his writing career in British television (contributing to *The Wednesday Play*, *Armchair Theatre* and *Play for Today*) and twice received Writers' Guild Awards. Movie credits include *The Return of the Soldier* (an adaptation of the novel by Rebecca West), Mel Brooks's production of *84 Charing Cross Road*, *Utz* (an adaptation of Bruce Chatwin's novel) and Franco Zeffirelli's *Jane Eyre*. His stage plays include *Stevie*, *Pack of Lies*, *Breaking the Code*, *The Best of Friends*, *It's Ralph*, *A Letter of Resignation*, *Disposing of the Body*, *God Only Knows* and a new version of Pirandello's *As You Desire Me*. These plays have been translated into many languages and produced throughout the world. Hugh Whitemore's work has twice been named Best Single TV Drama by the UK Broadcasting Press Guild; he has received the Scripter Award in Hollywood (for *84 Charing Cross Road*), the Script Prize at the 1998 Monte Carlo Festival (for his adaptation of *A Dance to the Music of Time*), a special Communications Award from the American Mathematical Society (for *Breaking the Code*), an Emmy Award for outstanding writing and the Writers' Guild of American Award (for *The Gathering Storm*). He is a Fellow of the Royal Society of Literature and an Honorary Fellow of King's College, London.

The Last Cigarette was first performed at the Minerva Theatre, Chichester, on 11 March 2009. The cast was as follows:

Simon 1 Jasper Britton
Simon 2 Nicholas Le Prevost
Simon 3 Felicity Kendal

Director Richard Eyre
Designer Rob Howell
Lighting and Projection Designer Jon Driscoll
Music George Fenton

THE LAST CIGARETTE

Act One

Three Simons, dressed identically, are sitting in identical
swivel chairs; but the effect of each is different, expressing
the different elements of their personalities. Simon 1 is
the thinker and serious questioner; he is comfortable
in his clothes, which are neat and unobtrusive. Simon 2
is more of a jeerer and a joker, anarchic, and there is a
touch of the slob about his appearance. Simon 3 is female,
and is elegantly and prettily dressed, a boy-girl, girl-boy,
but sometimes maternal.

SIMON 1

It's like this, at least in my imagination –

SIMON 3

you come back home one evening,

SIMON 1

the house is dark, as you expect it to be,

SIMON 2

you switch on a light,

SIMON 1

an extra light,

SIMON 3

one you didn't know you had,

SIMON 1

and unexpectedly your eye goes to a corner of the room
that you've never seen illuminated before,

SIMON 2

and in it is crouching a grinning man holding a knife –

SIMON 1

a grinning man

SIMON 2

holding a knife –

SIMON 3

a knife –

SIMON 2

grinning –

SIMON 1

and then the light goes off, normal lighting is resumed,
there is no one in the corner as far as you can see,

SIMON 3

but you know that if the light came on again you would
see him again,

SIMON 1

again

SIMON 3

in more detail,

SIMON 2

the teeth,

SIMON 3

one particular and prominent tooth,

SIMON 1

the completely confident intent in the eyes

SIMON 2

to murder you,

SIMON 1

and you can't get out of your house –

SIMON 3

once your protection and the most comforting place in the world –

SIMON 2

now your prison –

SIMON 3

inhabited by you and the creature in the corner,

SIMON 1

a grinning man holding a knife

SIMON 2

who might also be slipping into other rooms,

SIMON 3

to catch you there,

SIMON 1

or there,

SIMON 2

or there,

SIMON 3

in his own good time.

SIMON 1

So I am living in a state of terror and cowardice –

SIMON 2

I am waiting to be murdered in my own house by the grinning murderer with a knife.

SIMON 1

I almost want to give myself over to him – there,

SIMON 3

there you are, do it,

do it now –

but mostly I want to run and run, as if running will carry
me away from him, and not carry him along inside me,
there for the ride, enjoying it.

Enjoying it,

inside me.

Blackout.

*Lights up. Simon's study. There are books chaotically
everywhere, a desk with a typewriter on it and some
papers, another desk with an Apple Mac computer and
some yellow pads full of illegible writing; portraits on
the wall, Schubert and Dickens, a couple of cricketers
by Spy, a watercolour of a frog, but nothing exceptional,
pretty well what you'd expect of a man who does the
sort of things Simon does – except for the shoes, all
his shoes, which are lined up against the wall, about
twelve pairs, some of them worn only once or twice,
others he's used for over twenty years; there are
espadrilles with holes in the toes and flattened down
heels, sneakers and trainers and sandals.*

*Simon 1 is editing text on the Apple; Simon 2 is
writing in a yellow pad; Simon 3 is reading a book by
Stefan Zweig* (Beware of Pity). *All have Diet Cokes
within easy reach. A haze of cigarette smoke. Simon 1
takes a Silk Cut and lights it.*

Over the years I've developed a pattern of working
through most of the night and sleeping through most of

the morning. I generally go to bed at dawn and get up at lunchtime.

Victoria is generally in bed from about midnight to breakfast time.

This means I have my breakfast, a solitary breakfast, in the early afternoon, a really rotten time to breakfast at, especially if you find that you're not alone even though your wife is out, that there's a man you've never seen before moving about at the end of the hall, busy with implements. I decided he wasn't a burglar. A burglar would surely have taken me into account in some way, not just worked around me as I ate my breakfast and scanned the newspapers – then I saw a little note from Victoria on the table reminding me that the electrician might be around when I woke up. So that was all right then. I went to my study, calling out for George (dog). No George. Out with Victoria, I assumed.

George is in fact a bitch, though not in her sexual behaviour – she constantly attempts to rape our large fluffy black tom cat, neutered, whose name is Errol. Errol likes being raped by George, rolling about under her paws and even submitting occasionally to a brief sort of humping.

I gave one last call on the off chance – 'George!' – and was answered by the electrician. I went to the top of the stairs. He stood at the bottom, a youngish man, tall, dark haired. A touch public schooly in his posture, not threatening, but distinctly commanding. I was wearing my woolly dressing gown, making it difficult to be commanding back, even though I thought he was answering to my call for a dog.

SIMON 1
I need to look at your cheese board.

SIMON 2
That's what I heard him say. 'Cheeseboard? You want the cheese board?' In my half-asleep, half-awake state it didn't strike me as odd that an electrician should want to look at our cheese board, I've always accepted that any trade but my own has mysteries, but I felt oddly about it, if I can make this distinction – perhaps it was being in the woolly dressing gown at the head of the stairs – Barbara Stanwyck in *Double Identity* –

SIMON 3
Indemnity, you fool, *Double Indemnity*, Barbara Stanwyck making her entrance in a tight skirt, coming down the stairs in a tight skirt, was there a chain around her ankle, a light gold chain? Well, it's a ridiculous, not to say impertinent comparison with you at the top of the stairs in a woolly dressing gown, even if the electrician could have passed himself off as Fred McMurray, which he couldn't because of his overalls.

SIMON 2
He said what it was he wanted again, but this time the 'cheese' part of it was slurred. 'What board?' I said, 'What board?' coming halfway down the stairs.

SIMON 1
Fuse board.

SIMON 2
Fuse board! So I went on down the stairs, then down further stairs to the basement, to show him, after a prolonged search, where the fuse board wasn't. There were a lot of other boards there, burglar alarm boards,

telephone boards, boards to do with the television, so it was perfectly reasonable, in my view, to expect to find the fuse board among them. He went back up the basement steps ahead of me, darted into a room off the kitchen, and located the fuse board. As soon as I saw it I knew I'd known it was there all along. I'd been to it once or twice to press switches, which is all you have to do nowadays to change a fuse. The effect of this little encounter was to make me feel that I'd be better off fully dressed. So I put on my clothes and became a proper part of the day, a part of the day that was now actually beginning to fade.

The front doorbell rings. The Simons are suddenly alert, exchanging apprehensive glances.

SIMON 1
It must've been about eight o'clock, about the time when Victoria and I were vaguely preparing to cross the road to dinner at Chez Moi –

SIMON 3
There was a ring on the doorbell.

SIMON 2
We froze,

SIMON 3
she in her study,

SIMON 2
I in mine, waiting for the bell to ring again or for the bellringer to go away.

SIMON 3
We have a policy, since we were mugged on the pavement outside the house, never to answer the door in the evening unless we know for certain who's there. The bell didn't ring again.

9

SIMON 2
'Any idea who that might have been?' I bellowed huskily.

SIMON 3
(Pretty exact description – my voice, when used normally, is low and broken from fifty-seven years of smoking but when raised it comes out husky.)

SIMON 2
Did you get a look?

SIMON 3
No, she said, she'd seen a shape at the frosted glass in the front door, but couldn't tell anything, not even the sex, it had only been a glimpse, really, from the top of the stairs.

SIMON 1
I have a dread of policemen at the door, bearing bad news, a hangover from the years when my children were at that sort of stage – Lucy's first car, Ben coming home from school across the Archway Road, the busiest and vilest road in London –

SIMON 2
Well, did you get a sense? Did you hear the footsteps? Could it have been a policeman?

SIMON 3
Yes, it could have been a policeman, I suppose, it could have been anyone – I didn't really hear anything.

SIMON 1
I was suddenly convinced that I had, that I'd heard the heavy tread, with something slow and deliberate in it, of a policeman, though now I come to think of it it'd have to have been a policeman from another age, a policeman from *Dixon of Dock Green*, if not Dixon himself, the policemen of these days don't have a heavy tread, for one thing they don't wear constabulary boots, they wear light,

smart shoes that probably cause them to pitter-patter
lightly along, in twos or threes or even little packs of four
or five, towards some pop star whose internet habit they
are investigating – clearly, then, if I'd thought about it, the
heavy tread I hadn't heard hadn't belonged to a policeman,
but not having thought about it and now actually
assuming our bell had been rung by a policeman, actually
picturing him in his helmet, heavy jacket, enveloping
blue trousers, and his large boots, we crossed the road to
Chez Moi and saw, as we entered, Harold and Antonia
seated at a table facing the door, in the second room.

SIMON 2
Harold, Antonia, Victoria and I have dined at this table
for many years, in sickness and in health – and there's
the other table, the table for two, where Victoria and I
have spent some of our brightest and certainly our darkest
hours, my every birthday since we started together, and
there we sat after Victoria's mother's death, and after my
brother Piers's death,

SIMON 1
and it was crossing the road on our way to that table
that I proposed to Victoria.

SIMON 3
I came across a moment ago and rang your bell to see if
you wanted to join us,

SIMON 1
said Antonia.

SIMON 3
I saw somebody through the glass at the top of the stairs,
so I knew you were in.

SIMON 1
We reminded her of our policy of never answering the
door until we know who is there, without of course

explaining that I'd mistaken her tread, which I hadn't actually heard, for that of a policeman's from a distant epoch, but it struck me as unusual, not to say unprecedented, for her to have rung the doorbell, and there was something in Harold's manner, subdued and soft in his greetings.

SIMON 2
The thing is,

SIMON 3
he said, almost as soon as we'd sat down,

SIMON 2
I might as well tell you, I've just discovered – well, today in fact – that I've got cancer.

SIMON 3
And now a word from our sponsor!

SIMON 2
Simon Gray smokes Silk Cut. He is now smoking a Silk Cut. He is not feeling bilious. He has not just coughed. He is by no means on the verge of throwing up. He is as happy as a babe on the teat, and why not? as he cannot distinguish between mother's milk and nicotine, as long as he sucks, sucks.

SIMON 1
Did Mummy breast-feed anyway? I don't think so, I can't remember, although sometimes when I light a cigarette and suck in, I have a soothing, backwards-rolling feeling, and that I'm on the end of something life-sustaining, no, life-enhancing, almost as if it were unfiltered. Of course Mummy was a heavy smoker, so perhaps I was suckled on nicotine milk.

SIMON 3
You too can be suckled by Silk Cut. Five pounds a packet. Five pounds times three times a day equals £15

times seven equals £105 per week times fifty-two equals somewhere around £6,000 a year, wow!

SIMON 2

Is that all? All those headaches, phlegm-driven coughing fits, and rancid stomachs for only £6,000. And just think of all the things you can't get for £6,000!

SIMON 3

Thank you, Mummy!

SIMON 2

Yes – thank you, Mummy!

SIMON 3

I was the one she loved to fondle, the one she made sit on her lap, whose legs she stroked, whose hair she ruffled, the nape of whose neck she kissed, etc., and so forth, while Nigel and his father –

SIMON 2

well, my father too, our father, Nigel's and mine –

SIMON 1

but I tended to see them as a twosome –

SIMON 2

so there were two twosomes, Daddy and Nigel –

SIMON 3

Mummy and me.

SIMON 1

The Daddy and Nigel twosome stood or sat by with the appearance of disdain for all these displays of full-blooded passion – yes, that was it –

SIMON 2

Mummy and I were the adoring couple, Nigel and Daddy were a pair of disapproving relatives.

SIMON 1

And Piers – what about Piers? – over a decade younger than Nigel and me, and dead – how long is it now?

SIMON 2

Eight years, nine, ten.

SIMON 3

That long?

SIMON 2

The unfairness of it.

SIMON 3

On the day he was born –

SIMON 1

Whenever I remember it – the day he was born – it's always in a slack sort of way – Nigel then about twelve, myself ten and a bit. We're playing cricket on the pavement outside the house, and my mother –

SIMON 3

our mother –

SIMON 1

our mother – Nigel's and mine – comes out.

SIMON 2

She's wearing a hat, looking elegant and in a hurry.

SIMON 1

She stops, though, to announce with a smile that she's just given birth to a baby boy.

SIMON 3

We're going to call him Piers, isn't that exciting news? – now I'm off to meet Daddy, we haven't seen each other for such a long time –

SIMON 1

This is how the scene idles through my mind, and though

it's self-evidently wrong, it's always seemed right enough in feeling – actually, as I think about it properly, I see it's a conflation of two memories, the later one, to do with the announcement of Piers's birth mixed up with the early one, when I was about four and a half, Nigel six and three quarters therefore –

SIMON 2
we're playing in the snow outside our grandparents' house in Montreal,

SIMON 1
4047 Vendome Avenue.

SIMON 2
Our Aunt Gert – our father's sister – is in attendance somewhere but I can't see her in memory,

SIMON 3
all I see clearly is Mummy, dressed in her fur coat, carrying a small suitcase, walking hurriedly past us, her face averted.

SIMON 1
We ran over to her.

SIMON 2
Where are you going? Where are you going?

SIMON 3
I can't stop now, I'm going to get some milk.

SIMON 1
And off she went smiling a smile that meant something terrible. Aunt Gert told us to go indoors, where Grandma was waiting to tell us that the milk, so to speak, was back in England, with Daddy.

SIMON 2
So Daddy was the milk.

Mummy's milk.

The three explode into laughter. Cough.

SIMON 3

Yes, but Gert –

SIMON 1

Yes, poor old Aunt Gert –

SIMON 2

small, thin, wiry with a sharp voice, often irritable or
exasperated –

SIMON 1

yes, but doing her best –

SIMON 2

yes, doing her best –

SIMON 1

against the grain of her temperament and possibly
ambitions, to look after her brother's two children,

SIMON 2

for whom she had little natural affection –

SIMON 1

but towards whom she had a strong sense of duty.

SIMON 2

Unlike Grandma – full of affection, no sense of duty.

SIMON 3

I loved her and she loved me.

SIMON 2

She was so – so –

SIMON 1

Such a – such a –

SIMON 3

roly-poly, playful, laughing – sometimes hysterically
laughing – magnificat of a grandmother –

SIMON 1

perpetually sucking peppermints

SIMON 2

to conceal the sherry on her breath.

SIMON 1

Yes, but the point is – the point is –

SIMON 3

she adored me, and I adored being adored. By her. She
used to tickle me until I nearly fainted, bundle me about
the bed, and hold me into her breasts, enveloping me
with her wonderfully pepperminty smell. It was – it was
addictive.

SIMON 2

That was the sherry!

SIMON 1 *and* 3

It was Grandma!

SIMON 2
(*laughs*)

Yes, it was Grandma.

*They sit back, smoking, smiling reminiscently and
with pleasure.*

SIMON 2
(*with a little laugh*)

Poor old Grandpa.

SIMON 1

Yes, poor old Grandpa.

SIMON 3

Poor Grandpa,

so short and bow-legged, with his bristly grey crew-cut
and sticking-out ears and his Scots accent – still as strong
as the day he left Greenock, and all that energy –
bursting with it.

SIMON 1

And anger. Bursting with that, too –

SIMON 3

jealous anger!

SIMON 2

The truth is –

SIMON 3

was –

SIMON 1

poor old Grandpa wasn't wanted in the marital bed,

SIMON 3

and I was.

SIMON 1

So there he was, full of anger, jealousy and energy and
nowhere to put any of it. It, being Scots, Presbyterian,
faithful, honourable, etc. –

SIMON 3

except once, into me, with a strap.

SIMON 2

He was in some other room – his own bedroom, perhaps,
lying, staring at the ceiling, listening, listening to the
sounds –

SIMON 3

of me and Grandma frolicking on her bed. She would
order me to go and wash and brush my teeth and put on
my pyjamas and then say goodnight to Grandpa; I would

pretend to go, then dart back, slide under the bed,
reappear where least expected, allow her to catch me,
tickle me into helplessness –

SIMON 2
we were at it for hours, it must have seemed to Grandpa,
tormenting hours for him –

SIMON 3
blissful for me,

SIMON 2
and jolly, jolly, jolly for Grandma,

SIMON 1
the wife he was never not in love with, every second of
his life since he'd clapped eyes on her at a Greenock bus
stop.

SIMON 3
He erupted into the room, wielding a strap. He seized me
by the nape of the neck, ran me into his bedroom where
he swung me about with one hand, flailed at me with the
strap with the other, yelping out half-sentences to do
with teaching me to go to bed when I'm told – time I
learnt.

SIMON 1
Grandma stood at the door, swaying, pleading, crying out
with the blows:

SIMON 3
It's my fault, all my fault! – we were only playing! Stop,
James, please stop!

SIMON 2
And Aunt Gert, shocked and silent, grappling with
different duties and devotions – to the nephew to whom
she was an unwilling guardian, to a father she revered,
to a brother she worshipped –

of course, I didn't really know what she was grappling with, didn't know then (too busy with yelps, screams and sobs of my own).

SIMON 1
And soon after Nigel and I were sent back to England, some months before the war ended.

SIMON 2
I remember almost nothing about it – of the leave-taking, last cuddles, etc., nothing of the trip to New York, or of being put on the boat by Grandpa and Gert, of the journey itself, nothing,

SIMON 3
I remember Mummy's face, though, appalled –

SIMON 1
well, I mean, there standing before her were two little thugs, with crew-cuts and jug-ears and Canadian accents, come back in place of the English moppets she'd last seen outside 4047 Vendome Avenue, on her way to get the milk.

SIMON 2
From Grandma, Grandpa and Gert, Nigel and I got Christmas cards and birthday cards, five dollars inserted, until we'd grown up.

SIMON 1
To think we never saw them again.

SIMON 2
No, just a minute, there was that once –

SIMON 3
Yes, of course, when I was in my early twenties, stopped by for lunch on my way from London to Halifax, Nova Scotia. Grandma was in her late seventies –

SIMON I

Not much older than I am now!

SIMON 2

Christ, what a thought!

SIMON 3

There weren't any rollings about on the bed, or ticklings and hysteria, but there was still something in her eyes when she looked me over from top to toe, and then took my hands in hers and gave them a long, suggestive squeeze. Oh, I can tell from these hands you're a writer. These have never done a day's work in their life, and don't intend to.

SIMON I

Odd, isn't it, how they all died within months of each other, from unrelated illnesses,

SIMON 2

though not odd, really, when you think about it. Whichever went first was the crucial prop removed. The other two followed, of necessity.

SIMON I

Like a law of nature.

They get up and walk about.

SIMON I
(*sits down*)
What were we –? Oh, yes, well, where were we?

They look at each other, puzzled.

SIMON 3
(*snaps her fingers*)
Mummy. Mummy and her two thuggish sons who'd come back in place of the English moppets.

SIMON 1

So what were they like, those first days –? weeks –?
months?

SIMON 3

No idea.

SIMON 2

Haven't a clue.

SIMON 1

Well, let's think – the war was still going on – austerity,
cold, hunger, rationing – we were on Hayling Island so
there was the sea, Daddy was a doctor so there must
have been patients coming to the house, and school –

SIMON 2

we were sent to the only school on the island.

SIMON 3

A girls' school.

SIMON 2

To make us more English.

They laugh.

SIMON 1

But even so, no clear memories, not a single one –

SIMON 3

We were in shock.

SIMON 1

When did Mummy first hit me?

SIMON 2

It wasn't me, it was Nigel – it was about the – about the
rations, wasn't it?

SIMON 3

Yes – the rations.

SIMON 1

It was over lunch. There was so little of it, after Montreal,
and he said – what did he say? –

SIMON 3

He spoke for both of us.

SIMON 1

Good old Nigel!

SIMON 2

'We want to know if you're withholding our rations.'

SIMON 3

He actually used the word 'withholding'.

SIMON 1

I like to think I supplied him with it, but I don't think
I did, he came to it by himself, indignation and suspicion
possibly enlarging his vocabulary.

SIMON 2

I don't know whether Mummy took his use of the word
'withholding' into account when she responded to his
question with a crisp slap across his chops, or his
buttocks, depending on availability, and asked him,

SIMON 3

how did he dare! –

SIMON 1

he didn't, after that.

SIMON 2

So yes, there you have it, Mummy was a zestful slapper
and cuffer. The first blows were a shock as Gert never
hit,

SIMON 3

and Grandpa only on that one occasion, when of course
it was Grandma he was hitting, she the sinner, I merely

23

the sin, but for Mummy hitting was an instinctive action, that induced in us appropriately instinctive reactions.

SIMON I
We learnt to duck, bob, weave and skip, so that if she connected we came to accept it as our failure of reflex, just as if she missed she accepted it as her failure –

SIMON 2
I suppose these days a mother like Mummy would be spending a lot of time in the courts and jail even, but we live in exceptionally stupid days, nasty and stupid, in which phrases do the work not only of thinking but of feeling.

SIMON 3
'An innocent child,' we invariably say, when we all know somewhere in our systems that there isn't, and never has been, such a creature –

SIMON I
except for Mummy, of course, because 'innocent' is certainly the word for her oaths-and-blows style of parenting. It came to her perfectly naturally, and was therefore the naturally perfect way to regain full contact with her two sons, after all, when we'd last seen her, heading for the milk, I'd been nearly four, Nigel six – when we next saw her I was nearly nine and Nigel ten. Of the five years in which she wasn't a practising mother, she'd spent one and some months in hospital with tuberculosis, and the three and a bit before that driving an ambulance on the RAF station where my father was a medical officer – so she'd seen – they'd both seen – a number of wounded, dying and dead young men, and she'd nearly died herself –

SIMON 2
so a lot of life lived without us, a substantial gap in our relationship to fill, and her clouts, cuffs, smacks etc.

were an effective way of filling it. After the first assault, which took us by surprise and shocked us to tears, we enjoyed, no loved – loved, although we'd never have admitted it, but what was it we loved –?

SIMON 3
The intimacy, that was it, the knockabout intimacy of it. Within a month we were closer to her than we'd been to poor, undemonstrative Aunt Gert during the years of her dogged attentions.

SIMON 1
Our father didn't go in for cuffs and blows, such intimacy with his sons probably seemed unnatural to him –

SIMON 2
He beat us once, for reasons unremembered.

SIMON 3
Yes, why did he beat us? I can't think Nigel ever did anything worth a beating, and he never found out any of the things I should've been beaten for.

SIMON 1
Well, when was it?

SIMON 2
Must've been after we'd moved to London –

SIMON 1
before we went to our public schools; I to Sminster, Nigel to Spaul's.

SIMON 3
Thank God it wasn't the other way round, they played rugby at Spaul's –

SIMON 2
I know! – it was while we were at that ghastly little prep school in Putney, where there were two foul teachers,

Mr Brown, who was tall with bad teeth and beat me
incessantly, sometimes twice a day –

SIMON I
and Mr Burn, who was small and fat and had a husky
voice

SIMON 2
and hooded drowsy eyes

SIMON I
and put powder on his cheeks and shiny stuff on his lips

SIMON 3
and smelt of lemons, and cuddled me tenderly after every
one of Mr Brown's beatings.

SIMON 2
They worked as a team – each after his own pleasure –

SIMON 3
beatings cuddle, cuddle beating –

SIMON I
with some maths and Latin in between.

SIMON 2
Poor old Daddy, he didn't get any kind of pleasure from
the one beating, not even the pleasure of being stern and
manly.

SIMON I
His heart wasn't in it. He did it almost shyly –

SIMON 3
with a floppy slipper –

SIMON 2
though he made us bend down –

SIMON 3
but not touching our toes, just arms hanging vaguely
down, bums sticking vaguely out, whisking the floppy

slipper across our short-trousered buttocks, as if he were dusting them.

SIMON 1

Imitating the way a schoolmaster did it.

SIMON 2

Actually not at all like being beaten at school.

SIMON 3

That had ceremony and drama. I didn't enjoy the pain, but I more than enjoyed the distinction it conferred on me, moving amongst my peers, my bum smarting but my head held high; not a manly figure, nor a boyish one, something decidedly girlish, possibly – a punished princess, yes, the sexual thrill came not with the beating, but after it, in a delicious sense of how I was being perceived, perceiving myself as a self perceived, honoured, desired –

SIMON 1

which is not, of course, how I may have been perceived at all; contemptuously or disgustedly may have been how I was perceived –

SIMON 2

depending on the sexual and emotional make-up of the perceivers, some of whom were no doubt capable of complicated combinations of contempt, lust, disgust etc. for posturing and knowing fourteen-year-olds. (*Laughs.*) I can't imagine strutting titillatingly about like a captive princess after Daddy's beating –

SIMON 3

Mummy would have slapped her out of us in a jiffy –

SIMON 1

Who do you think you are, you little fool, you look quite disgusting, with your bottom sticking out and pouting

like some silly girl and it's rude to your father, after all
the trouble he's gone to, to make a man of you!

Simons 1 and 2 laugh.

SIMON 3
She wasn't like that. Not really.

SIMON 2
No, but she's become like that. In our memory.

SIMON 1
Only sometimes. Other times – lots of other times – I
remember her – (*A gesture.*)

SIMON 3
With love, of course.

SIMON 2
When I think of her, that is.

SIMON 1
Anyway, I was thinking about Daddy. How beating –
violence – just not in his nature.

SIMON 2
No, he did his damage in little asides I could only just
hear –

SIMON 3
Like the time he asked me what I was reading and I said
The Ballad of Reading Gaol.

SIMON 1
Who's that by?

SIMON 3
Oscar Wilde.

SIMON 2
As he left the room his words drifted back into it, like
his pipe smoke –

SIMON 1

Sickening little pansy.

SIMON 2

So much for Oscar Wilde.

SIMON 1

Sickening little pansy.

SIMON 3

Unless he meant me, of course.

SIMON 1

Just the normal philistine response of his period –

SIMON 3

Our period.

SIMON 1

Good old nineteen fifties.

SIMON 2

But there was something else in him –

SIMON 3

The wellington boots!

SIMON 2

God, yes, the wellington boots.

SIMON 1

Wellington boots?

SIMON 3

We came out of the house one Sunday to go for a spin
in the car, it was raining and Mummy said, 'Why aren't
you wearing your wellies, you fool? Go and put on your
boots!'

SIMON 2

This to me, not to her husband.

SIMON 3
I don't want to wear my wellies – I hate wearing my wellies! They're too tight and too heavy!

SIMON 1
Do as you're told! Go and get them!

SIMON 2
So down I went to the basement, plucked out my wellies, and discovered a gash in the heel of one of them. 'Unwearable, they're unwearable,' I said, showing them the boot.

SIMON 3
'How on earth did that happen?' she said, not conspicuously perplexed.

SIMON 2
'I don't know,' I said, not particularly curious.

SIMON 1
'He did it himself,' said the father, not at all himself. Steely with anger.

SIMON 2
No, Mummy, I didn't. Honestly.

SIMON 1
And honestly I hadn't.

SIMON 3
No, he wouldn't have. He wouldn't be so bloody silly, would you darling?

SIMON 1
He did it himself. He's lying. Look at his shifty little eyes.

SIMON 2
'His shifty little eyes.' Now this was said not of the moment – he didn't mean that my eyes at that precise moment, in circumstances to do with my boots, were

30

shifting about, but as a general moral fact about me, my eyes were always shifty, I'd been born with shifty eyes as an indicator of my true nature – eyes-as-windows-of-the-soul shifty.

SIMON 1

Mummy, my mummy, was shocked.

SIMON 3

James!

SIMON 1

she cried, cried Mummy mine.

SIMON 3

James, how could you!

SIMON 2

He muttered something apologetic – his own eyes suddenly shifty and full of feeling.

SIMON 1

What feeling?

SIMON 2

Loathing would be to take it too far, I think, looking judiciously back, but whatever it was it gave me, in all my upset, a little jolt of triumph.

SIMON 3

I was walking home from school. I must've been about fifteen. It was somewhere in Pimlico, mid-afternoon, I was about to cross a street and they went past in a car, my father and Little Mrs Rolls; she was driving, my father sitting staring straight ahead, a perfectly proper little cameo, really.

SIMON 2

She was a small, blonde, lively widow, who worked as Daddy's secretary in his Harley Street consultancy –

'Little Mrs Rolls,' my mother invariably referred to her as, or, in poignant innocence – 'Your Little Mrs Rolls.'

SIMON 3
Your Little Mrs Rolls phoned to say she's made three appointments for you on Wednesday afternoon.

SIMON 2
One of them, possibly two, even all three, being with Little Mrs Rolls herself, it was subsequently discovered.

SIMON 1
So there they were, in a Pimlico street – a small blonde secretary driving her boss to one of his appointments. They weren't laughing, talking, looking at each other, they might've been in separate vehicles from the evident lack of connection between them – perhaps that was the trouble, perhaps that's what I unconsciously grasped, the unlikely stiffness and formality with which they sat – especially him, he gave off the impression of being somehow both lordly and a captive.

SIMON 3
Or did he? That may be how I see him now, in memory.

SIMON 1
But what I did notice at the time is that they sat, both of them, as if they were hoping not to be observed by someone that they themselves had observed –

SIMON 2
to wit: myself –

SIMON 1
well, whether they were or they weren't because they had or they hadn't, the thing is, without actually knowing anything at all, really, about adultery, unfaithfulness, all that, I knew that I'd seen something wrong, that I'd caught him out, and I didn't like it. That's why I didn't

mention it to Mummy or to Nigel – perhaps I felt it'd be
sneaking, even though I didn't understand yet what it
was I'd be sneaking about.

SIMON 2
The truth was revealed some months later.

SIMON 3
Mummy asked me to come with her, for a drive. We
went to the car and sat in it. She didn't start the car, we
just sat there, in the car, in front of the house. She told
me about Little Mrs Rolls and my father – 'your father'
was her term for him on this occasion, instead of the
usual 'Daddy' – she cried a bit, said she'd thought of
leaving him. It had been going on for eight years, she
said, and she'd never for a moment suspected. And then
she said, 'But why should I leave him? Why should I
give up everything because of her? Why should I let her
ruin my life, destroy my family? Why should I give her
that satisfaction?'

SIMON 1
And this conversation – how did it end?

SIMON 3
I think – I think –

SIMON 2
She suddenly remembered she had to take a hockey class.

SIMON 3
That's right. Her hockey class.

SIMON 2
So I got out and she drove off in her usual harum-scarum
way, cigarette dangling –

SIMON 3
The next day she reported crisply that Daddy –

your father, she said –

SIMON 3
your father has written to Little Mrs Rolls – a letter that
requires – no, demands – no reply, so there's nothing
more to be said – we'll never mention the matter again,
Si, darling. It was wrong of me to have burdened you
with it, your father's a good man and he loves me – he
loves us all.

SIMON 1
And almost immediately there was laughter again from
their bedroom that I sometimes caught when I was up
early. I was, well, relieved that Father was in his proper
place, about his proper business, but I had, there's no
getting away from it, a most peculiar mixture of new
feelings for him – a respect for his 'otherness', that to
himself he was obviously far more than father, husband,
pathologist.

SIMON 2
He had a secret life, just like me, he had desires and
needs, just like me, but unlike me he knew how to satisfy
them –

SIMON 3
he was a grown-up, in other words he knew how to
deceive. Eight years –

SIMON 1 *and* 2
eight years! –

SIMON 1
he was or had been a betrayer.

SIMON 2
And don't forget Bunty, Mummy's best friend, and
Daddy's best friend's wife – Nigel surprised them when

he came home from school early one afternoon, met them on the landing coming out of the bedroom –

SIMON 3

out of Mummy's bedroom is how I see it –

SIMON 2

both of them flushed, holding just-lit cigarettes, and Daddy, devious old devil, said, 'Just showing Mrs Marus something in the bedroom.'

SIMON 1

'Mrs Marus.' That's how one's parents referred to their closest friends, when in their company in front of the children – to each other it was Bunty this, Bunty that, but to the children:

SIMON 2

Just showing Mrs Marus something in the bedroom.

SIMON 3

Mrs Marus was onomatopoeically a Bunty: a large, round, soft, horsey, chuckling sort of woman, as tall as Mummy, but with enormous breasts –

SIMON 2

boobs, actually –

SIMON 3
(laughs)

Yes, boobs.

SIMON 2

Poor old Mummy, flat-chested Mummy, used to say proudly, 'Mrs Marus worships your father,' not knowing, to her dying day where and how or with what . . .

SIMON 3

So Daddy – Daddy –

SIMON 1

my father –

SIMON 2

did I love him?

They all light cigarettes.

SIMON 3
(*after a pause*)

Did I love him?

SIMON 2

Love?

SIMON 1

Love him?

SIMON 3

We sat, he and I sat hand-in-hand in some obscure nook in the Abbey Cloisters.

SIMON 2

Hand-in-hand? Did I really?

SIMON 1

His name was Robert. Robert Symonds.

SIMON 2

One 'm' or two?

SIMON 1

One. One I think.

Simon 3 has written the name on a yellow pad; he passes it to Simon 1; Simon 2 looks over his shoulder.

SIMON 2

Yes, two then. Sym-monds.

SIMON 1

How quaint it seems, how quaint the image, two full-grown boys, tall and well built, in their school suits that weren't quite uniforms, a liberal school prescribing only the colours but not the shades or the textures of the trousers and jackets, and allowing some slight variations in the cut, but then there were the stiff white collars, big black shoes – so if not uniforms then a general sense of uniformity, and of uniform clumsiness, yes, that was it, so clumsily dressed we were, or dressed to make us seem clumsy, as we sat on a stone bench or the lid of a tomb, generally in the late afternoon, our hands intertwined, Robert Symmonds and I, talking about our feelings not for but about each other.

SIMON 2

What is this distinction?

SIMON 1

I suppose I mean that our conversation, sometimes tremulous, sometimes savage, nevertheless moved in speculations and observations,

SIMON 3

The thing about you, Simon –

SIMON 1

and

SIMON 3

I often wonder, Robert, why you –

SIMON 1

rather than:

SIMON 3

When I see you in the Yard, waiting for me, my heart dips with apprehension and longing. It's because I love you.

SIMON 2

Love me, what do you love about me?

SIMON 3
I love – I love –

SIMON 1
What did I love about him? That he was mysterious, unpredictable, would suddenly snatch his hand from mine, get up and walk away, standing with his head bowed, as if in despair at the company he was keeping, while I would sit staring at him hopelessly.

SIMON 3
I could never go to him and touch him and say, 'What's the matter? What have I done? How can I put it right? Please forgive me.'

SIMON 1
It would've been a breach of something I couldn't formulate then and still can't understand.

SIMON 3
Let me think . . .

SIMON 1
Perhaps going to him and touching him would've had too many possible meanings –

SIMON 3
and to touch him where? on the shoulder, like a policeman? – it would've been a trespass, in the sense of entering dangerous and forbidden ground.

SIMON 2
On the other hand it might've been cowardice, a fear that any gesture I made would be met with contempt, or a complete departure –

SIMON 3
Perhaps he wanted me to go to him and touch him, the more meanings in the touch the better – at least he was still there, averted but present, and would return,

SIMON I

I prayed that he would return –

SIMON 2

Usually he did, in fact he always did.

SIMON I

He'd come back and sit down and say,

SIMON 2

in his loud offhand voice,

SIMON I

something that amused him, and he would follow it with
a loud, forced laugh,

SIMON 3

and our hands would touch, enfold, fingers intertwining.

SIMON I

How odd it seems now, the intensity of those meetings,
how odd that I remember the feelings so strongly, but
can't recall a single conversation, a single sentence from
any of our conversations, although I remember the
content, which he mainly provided –

SIMON 2

Sartre, Man Ray, Cocteau, etc., and of course my sporting
life, how incomprehensible he found it that I should spend
afternoons playing football or cricket, it was a joke to
him, though not one that he much enjoyed because it
was also treason, all those hours when I could have been
doing something intelligent, by which he meant being
with him, in the cloisters where we could hold hands, or
in the library, where we could sit together in the
armchairs.

SIMON I

And of course we talked about his impending death – he
said that he'd be lucky to live until he was twenty; he'd

certainly be dead before he was twenty-five. Of course I didn't believe him, although I wanted to, death being a great and romantic adventure that seemed almost an aspiration.

SIMON 2

Yes, I thought it was a boast, really, and admired him for its extravagance, because death was also something that didn't actually happen, at least to anybody one knew, apart from elderly relatives, who had been alive one month, and then were dead by post the next.

SIMON I

He was at Oxford, in his second or third year, I'd just come back from France – all I remember is the phone call to his house, his mother's voice on the line. She said, 'I'm afraid he's not here, Simon – he's in hospital, it's his stomach – his stomach again.' I asked her when she thought he would be out.

SIMON 3

She said, 'Well I'm not sure – he's very ill, I'm afraid, very, very ill.'

SIMON I

Then she told me which hospital he was in and asked me to visit him. 'He'd love to see you,' she said.

SIMON 3

He'd love to see you.

SIMON 2

The thought of Robert, in a hospital, dying – it was too complicated, dark and grown-up a thought, I couldn't allow it in properly. I talked to several friends from school who had been with Robert at Oxford and who visited him in hospital.

SIMON I

Prepare yourself for a shock, he's very thin, you almost

won't recognise him – but there's still something about
him that's Robert –

SIMON 3
the smile of course, and the way his eyes light up when
he sees you, he doesn't seem to mind that he's dying,
that's the most Robert part of him, so exactly Robert –
he'll be so glad to see you, you and he were always so
close.

SIMON 1
I set out one day, in fear and trembling. I can't remember
how far I got, but it was nothing like far enough –

SIMON 2
I think I knew before I set out that I wasn't going to
arrive. Nor did I phone the hospital, or his mother, or
his friends, to find out how he was doing, whether there
was any chance, a reversal of fortune, or something of
the sort . . .

SIMON 1
Suppose he recovered, how would I be able to meet his
eye, explain my failure to see him when we all thought
he was dying?

SIMON 2
I could imagine him telling me that really it had been a
test and I'd failed it.

SIMON 1
If it did, in fact, feel like a test, it was because I knew I'd
failed – I was ashamed, but the shame wasn't as strong
as my fear, I could live with my shame if it meant not
having to see him, it was a price willingly paid, I was in
that respect in complete sympathy with myself.

SIMON 2
The truth is, I'd rather have died than seen Robert when
he was dying, it would have been far less taxing, I could

coast through my own death, which was after all unimaginable,

SIMON I

though his came to pass whether I'd imagined it or not. I made it to the funeral. I remember absolutely nothing about it. Surprising, really, as it was my first.

SIMON 3

My first love too . . .

SIMON 2

Pretty conventional really. A crush. It turns up in most lives.

SIMON I

In literature too, of course. Hamlet and Horatio, Antonio and Bassanio, Copperfield and Steerforth –

SIMON 3

Batman and Robin.

SIMON 2

What?

SIMON I

Where did that come from?

SIMON 2

Yes, what have we here?

SIMON I

It just popped out.

SIMON 3

I wanted to be Robin being saved by Batman.

SIMON I

Not always though, sometimes I wanted to be Batman saving Robin.

SIMON 2

Or both at once.

SIMON 3

The love that dare not speak its name.

SIMON 1

Not that I knew its name.

SIMON 3

So much easier when I grew up, and entered my manhood.

SIMON 1

Entered my manhood!

SIMON 2

Entered my manhood!

Simon 1 and 2 laugh, repeating 'Entered my manhood'.

SIMON 3

Well, I mean wanted women. Just like Daddy.

SIMON 1

Wanted women just like Daddy?

SIMON 2

Not many of those around.

Simon 1 and 2 laugh.

SIMON 1
(*stops laughing abruptly*)

But who was the first?

SIMON 3

Yes, my first woman, who was she?

They think.

SIMON 2

Esther.

SIMON 3

Esther . . . ?

SIMON 2

That was her name. Esther.

SIMON 1

I think there was something in front of it – Emma Esther.

SIMON 2

Sounds wrong.

SIMON 3

Anne – or Anesta

SIMON 1

Anita! It was Anita!

SIMON 2

Am I sure?

SIMON 3

No, Anesta. A-N-E-S-T-A . . .

SIMON 2

Anesta, Anita. Did I love her? That's the question.

SIMON 1

I remember anger, bitterness, hopelessness, despair, so yes.

SIMON 2

Did she love me?

SIMON 1

Yes. Until –

SIMON 2

Until?

SIMON 1

We had sex.

SIMON 2

Bad sex, then?

SIMON 1

No, worse than that.

SIMON 2

Can I be more precise?

SIMON 1

Well, actually it was no sex – a lot of physical activity but no actual sex.

SIMON 2

More precise!

SIMON 1

I peeled my trousers down to my knees and rolled my underpants down to my trousers' crotch. Then I lay on top of her and bucked about, yelping.

SIMON 2

Why?

SIMON 1

I didn't know what else to do. I was a virgin.

SIMON 2

A twenty-five-year-old virgin?

SIMON 3

That's right.

SIMON 2

Unusual, surely?

SIMON 1

I don't know. Possibly. Possibly not. This was 1961, don't forget, before the Beatles' first LP and so forth.

SIMON 2

And so I was anatomically ignorant?

45

Yes.

But I'm a doctor's son.

Yes.

Couldn't I have consulted a book?

I did, but it didn't make much sense.

I suppose I could have copied a diagram but I could scarcely have it in my hand when I got on top of her, like a road map.

Did she know I was a virgin?

No.

Would it have been better if I'd told her?

I expect so, because the next time she showed me what I was expected to do, and how and where to do it, by the end I would really have enjoyed it if she hadn't hated it so much.

Why did she hate it?

Probably never got over our first time, my first time, to be exact, she never got over my first time – she liked older men, really, older than herself and much older than me – men who took charge and ran the show. Even when I got used to it, I never ran the show, I got into the habit of waiting for instructions.

SIMON 2

Not a flyaway beginning, then.

SIMON 1

Still, it taught me some important things about – well, love.

SIMON 3

Love?

SIMON 2

Taught you about love?

SIMON 1

Yes.

SIMON 3

Well then, did you love him?

SIMON 1

Robert Symmonds?

SIMON 2

No.

They are all smoking. They all cough. Pat their chests. Wheeze. Cough again.

SIMON 1

You know, if this keeps up – (*Wheezes.*)

SIMON 3

I'm seriously thinking I'll have to – have to – (*Wheezes.*)

SIMON 2

to change my brand.

They burst into laughter, wheeze, then a pause.

SIMON 3
What about Daddy? Did you love my daddy?

SIMON 2
Did I love our daddy . . . ?

SIMON I
All I know is – all I can say is that –(*Little pause.*) –we
were swimming one summer afternoon on Hayling
Island, Mummy, Daddy, Nigel and I. All four of us were
in the water, all four of us were very good swimmers.

SIMON 3
It was Grandpa who taught me to swim in the lakes, in
Canada. Held me firmly under my stomach, encouraged
me to kick and to strike out with my arms – this wasn't
for graceful or stylish swimming, strictly functional, for
survival – the moment when he let me go and I didn't for
once flounder and sink, but remained in the water, held
up by my own mysterious forces and moving an inch or
two was the most ecstatic of my life.

SIMON I
The sea was calm that summer afternoon on Hayling
Island, and we moved about in it in a little family pack
until I found myself swimming away, heading out to sea
as fast as I could until I was out of my depth, and then
swam a bit further, and a bit further, the sea got colder,
my body weaker, until I couldn't swim any more.

SIMON 2
The waves seemed to be rolling inside my head, I started
to shake, pawing feebly at the water as I slipped under
it, and the next thing I was in his arms. Daddy'd kept
an eye on me when I'd struck out, noticed the growing
feebleness of my stroke, swum after me, gathered me in,
carried me to shore. He laid me on a towel, Mummy
poured tea from the Thermos down my throat –

SIMON 3
'Make sure it's got a lot of sugar in it,' my daddy said.

SIMON 1
Mummy asked, 'What happened?'

SIMON 3
'Nothing,' said Daddy. 'He got a little cold, and out-swam his strength, didn't you, old chap?'

SIMON 1
What has remained with me all my life was the feeling I had when I lay in his arms, my head against his chest – I was his child.

SIMON 2
Mummy died when she was fifty-eight.

SIMON 3
Don't go yet, Si, stay a little longer.

SIMON 2
She'd seen me looking at my watch: a swift, casual glance down at my wrist.

SIMON 1
I have to pick up Ben from his nursery school.

SIMON 2
She held out her hand to retain me. I held it to my lips, kissed her quickly on the forehead and left.

SIMON 1
Why didn't I stay? A few more minutes, that's all she wanted. It wasn't coldness of the heart or fear of seeing her so extremely ill and dying. There had just been an undeniable impulse to remove myself. Inexplicable.

SIMON 2
Every so often when she was in the middle of a lively sentence, there was a look in her eyes, vague and appalled – the words would stop and she would lie back –

her arms and legs had become sticks, her face gaunt, her eyes sunk, and her stomach. 'My dear, how ridiculous! I look pregnant!'

SIMON 1
But she maintained her belief that she would shortly become well right up to the last days, when she was given enough morphine to keep her either comatose or hallucinatory. In one of her last lucid spells she said,

SIMON 3
'I'll tell you one thing, Si, I've learnt my lesson. I'm never going to smoke another cigarette.'

SIMON 1
Daddy never learnt his. He died in the same hospital – Charing Cross – under the supervision of the same doctor.

SIMON 2
One afternoon I came in to find him agitated, knotting the end of his sheet with his fingers, turning his face one way and the other on his pillow, muttering. When I asked him what was up, was he OK, he wouldn't answer at first, then finally whispered that they'd taken his cigarettes, he didn't know what to do to get them back. I asked the matron where his cigarettes were.

SIMON 3
'Well,' she said, 'We think his smoking probably contributed to his illness.'

SIMON 1
But you say he's dying.

SIMON 2
Yes, he's dying.

SIMON 1
Then why not let him have his cigarettes?

SIMON 2

Because they're bad for him.

SIMON 1

But if he's dying –

SIMON 2

Because he smoked.

SIMON 1

But what does that matter now?

SIMON 2

It matters because he shouldn't smoke.

SIMON 1

And so forth, for quite some time, until I took it up
with the doctor – an old friend of my father's – who
countermanded the matron's orders. I sat beside him and
held his free wrist as he smoked the first of his recovered
cigarettes. He gave me such a smile, a smile of such
gratitude, that I felt I'd at last become a son to him, and
a bit of a father too.

SIMON 2

He died the following afternoon.

SIMON 3

Teatime the following afternoon.

SIMON 1

Piers was with me, at the bedside. He must have been
about twenty.

SIMON 3

Nineteen – he was nineteen – his first year at Cambridge,
so nineteen –

SIMON 2

And Nigel – was he there?

SIMON 1

Not quite, he was late – he was working in Montreal
and the plane was late.

SIMON 2

That's right.

SIMON 3

He arrived about five minutes after Daddy had gone.

SIMON 2

That's right.

SIMON 1

The three of us stood around his bed, wondering what to
do, what exactly was the procedure, etc.

SIMON 2

Then a nurse arrived with a tray of food.

SIMON 3

'Eat it all up,' she said.

SIMON 2

She put it down beside his bed and flashed him a nursey
smile.

SIMON 3

'Make sure he does. He needs it,' she said.

SIMON 1

They took him away eventually, and we took away the
things he'd had beside his bed, his spectacles, a book, his
pack of cigarettes, and a rather bulky gold lighter – a
present, I suppose, from someone or other. Poor Daddy.

SIMON 2

And yet – I still don't know whether I loved him . . .

SIMON 3

After all these years? Oh but, surely. I mean – I'm almost

the age he was when he died. Surely I must know by now whether I loved him?

SIMON 1
Well, the word itself, you know, the word love itself – (*Gestures hopelessly.*)

They get up, walk aimlessly around, smoking.

SIMON 2
The first person I knew I loved – the very first person I actually knew I actually loved –

SIMON 3
Piers of course. But that was easy. He was born when I was ten years old.

SIMON 2
Easy to love such a younger brother.

SIMON 3
Nothing complicated. Just big brother–little brother stuff.

SIMON 1
Every morning he would crawl to the top of the stairs, then manoeuvre himself down them in traditional baby style, bumping from step to step, three flights, on his bottom, crawl to the front door, pick up the morning's post, post it through a gap in the floorboards, would crawl into my bedroom, climb onto the bottom of the bed, and bounce on my feet until I woke up – I was already half-awake, actually, because I always knew he was there and would kick him gently up and down in harmony with his bouncing, giving him a little extra propulsion so he went a little higher, and a little higher, laughing drowsily with his gurgles and cries of joy, higher and higher I kicked and he bounced, until one morning I gave him a little too much extra propulsion and my kick bounced him off the bed.

SIMON 2

Was there intention?

SIMON 1

Well, there was something –

SIMON 2

malevolent?

SIMON 1

Yes, there was something malevolent working in me
through the drowsiness, not an impulse to hurt but to do
something unexpected, that would change the mood and
rhythm of the game, I wanted to surprise him and shock
him, this trusting, devoted two-year-old whom I adored,
to make the game suddenly my game and not his.

SIMON 2

He landed on the wooden floor on his head.

SIMON 3

It made a sound, soft but distinct.

SIMON 2

Baby Piers's baby skull.

SIMON 1

He lay there still, his face a white I'd never seen before.

SIMON 3

His eyes were closed. I picked him up, put him on the
bed, and begged him to wake up.

SIMON 2

Nothing happened,

SIMON 3

no colour in his cheeks,

SIMON 1

his eyes sealed.

SIMON 3

I ran around the room crying and pleading, oh God, please God, please God, please! Please bring him back!

SIMON 1

I picked him up and clutched him to me.

SIMON 2

He was soft and dead in my arms.

SIMON 1

I put him down on the bed. I think what was going through me was this:

SIMON 3

that I loved him overwhelmingly, more than I had ever loved anyone, and that I'd killed him and would have to be punished, but that the punishment didn't matter as the world was no longer the place it had been moments before, moments before it had been a glorious and comfortable place and there was nothing I could do that would ever get me back into it – I must now go upstairs with dead Piers in my arms and present him to Daddy and Mummy, and the new world of punishment without Piers would begin.

SIMON 1

I remember quite clearly how I bent to pick him up from the bed,

SIMON 2

just as he let out a mewl, and opened his eyes,

SIMON 1

blinked,

SIMON 2

saw me,

SIMON 1

and gurgled.

SIMON 3

Oh, the smell of him when I had him in my arms, the sweet, soft life in him,

SIMON 1

it was without doubt the purest flood of emotion, the least complicated, the simplest flood of gratitude and love I had ever known, would ever know, ever.

SIMON 2

Five or six years later, we quarrelled so violently that he seized a carving knife, and threw it at me.

SIMON 1

'He threw the carving knife at me!' I said, when our mother came to find out what all the noise was about.

SIMON 2

He could've killed me!

SIMON 3

You could have killed me, Piers!

SIMON 1

I can't remember what the quarrel was about, but whatever it was, I was entirely in the wrong – how couldn't I have been, as I was sixteen or seventeen, and he was six or seven, and from my point of view he was mine to control, and from his, he wasn't.

SIMON 2

In his early drinking days, at Cambridge, he drank to be merry, sociable and free, he drank because he liked the taste, he drank because – well, why not?

SIMON 1

When he started teaching, he drank for the same reasons, and because it was what they all did in the Senior Common Room, but as the years went by he drank more and more, from frustration and anger and then despair, more and more, eventually scheduling his day around his bottle. Every term his condition got worse, until finally he was incapable of teaching, became a nuisance in the common room, was banned from the campus, invalided out.

SIMON 2
In his last weeks he would come round and sit silently in a chair in my study, his drink in his hand, his bottle of bourbon at his feet.

SIMON 3
His face, though, was unlined, his blue eyes clear and alert – it was a beautiful face, that I had used to gaze at in wonder and joy when it was a baby's, and would now glance at surreptitiously, nearly fifty years on. Occasionally he would catch my glance, smile with a serenity that seemed to have a taunt in it, raise his glass to his mouth – and I would turn back to my typewriter, clackety-clackety.

SIMON 2
When he was in his last clinic some friends came in a group to tell him that they could no longer bear witness to his self-destruction. If he didn't stop drinking, at least for a while, they would close their doors on him. He replied that he was sorry, but he couldn't contemplate life without alcohol. There was a long silence, and then one of them said,

SIMON 1
Well, Piers, you've just announced the end of our friendship.

SIMON 3
A few weeks later he collapsed with a burst liver, burst kidneys, burst everything, really.

His death caught him by surprise, I think – I certainly don't think he intended it, even though he did it by his own hand –

SIMON 1
but perhaps he had no choice, who knows?

SIMON 2
He certainly behaved as if he thought he hadn't, and all in all I'm pretty sure he wanted to go on living,

SIMON 1
if only to go on drinking.

SIMON 3
'Beloved' is the word I had put on his tombstone. He's buried in Kensal Green Cemetery, in Rowan Gardens, a new section, pastoral and domestic in feeling, with its own little gate. I've become very fond of it. 'Beloved.' When I sit on the bench opposite his grave and look at the word, it no longer seems simple and eloquent, but brutal and pretentious. I used to distract myself from it by getting up and walking around for a while, and then pausing in front of one of the graves eight down from Piers, on the right, as you face him. The headstone is rather jaunty, yellowy-grey in colour, with a photograph of a young man embedded in a little glass dome at the top. He is bareheaded, dark hair cut short, round, handsome face with slightly childlike features, unformed anyway, as if he hasn't grown into them yet. He is dressed in shiny black leather, mounted on a powerful motorbike, a helmet under one arm, the other resting on the handlebars.

SIMON 1
I worked out from his dates that he was just two days short of thirty-three years and one month old when he smashed himself up on the motorbike. One afternoon

when I was visiting I became interested in this question of ages, how long the dead in Piers's vicinity had spent in the world. I suppose I must have checked on about fifteen gravestones, and found two, both men, on which the arithmetic worked out at forty-nine – the age Piers was when he died. Altogether three out of sixteen, if one included Piers – must be unusual, surely, a freak clustering –

SIMON 2

'Clustering' . . .? Is that the right word?

Simon 3's mobile phone rings. She takes it out of her pocket and turns upstage to answers it. The other two take no notice.

SIMON 3
(on phone)

Hello? Hello?

Simon 1 is writing in his yellow pad. He stops for a moment.

SIMON 1

I'm looking down at my hand moving across the yellow pad, 'this warm scribe, my hand' –

SIMON 2

I don't know what to make of it, actually, my hand – I've had it all my life, couldn't be more familiar with it, know it like the back of my hand, etc.,

Simon 3 puts the phone back in her pocket.

SIMON 1

but suddenly it doesn't look like mine at all, with its liver spots, wrinkles over the knuckles, a getting-on-in-life, down-at-heel sort of hand . . .

SIMON 2

Who was that on the phone?

SIMON I

Certain events happen annually – Christmas, birthdays, wedding anniversaries – things that have to be observed, and in early July, for the last ten years, there have been the medical tests. I've come to treat them as irritating interruptions, as a formality that has nothing to do with how I actually feel – and why not? Every year the results have been pretty much the same, the sort of problems that have to do with age – cancer of the prostate, but so far it's still in the prostate, an aneurysm that has to be measured and will one day have to be operated on, but not yet – neither prostate nor aneurysm is treated by the doctors as alarming, and neither is thought about much by me –

SIMON 2

I regard the tests as a once–a–year humdrummery, and they still seem so this year, although the blood test shows cancerous activity – my GP and my urologist both assume that it's the prostate cancer stirring at last, but I'm not to worry, they're prepared, they know what has to be done. So I went for a scan that will show what the prostate is up to, and also a scan to show how the aneurysm is doing, and also a scan to make sure that there's no cancer in my bones – this was roughly the order, I think, and I was having the bone scan, an exceedingly boring business . . .

SIMON I

I was very tired on the afternoon of the scan, for some reason, but pleased to be so because I fell into a light doze, and stayed there until a disembodied voice roused me with the news that I was done. I got off the bed, put on my clothes, and stumbled out, still a bit sleepy, leaden-limbed and ill at ease. I spotted Victoria standing by a door at the top of the stairs, listening on her mobile. She saw me just as the conversation was evidently finished. (*Turning to Simon 3.*) Who was that on the phone?

Simon 3 takes both their hands, and turns first to Simon 1.

SIMON 3
They've found something in our lung. (*To Simon 2.*) On the aneurysm scan.

SIMON 1
What they call an 'opportunistic' finding.

SIMON 2
It's like this, at least in my imagination, you come back home one evening, the house is dark, as you expect it to be, you switch on a light, an extra light, one you didn't know you had, and unexpectedly your eye goes to a corner of the room that you've never seen illuminated before, and in it is crouching a grinning man holding a knife – and then the light goes off, normal lighting is resumed, there is no one in the corner a far as you can see, but you know that if the light came on again you would see him again, see him in more detail, the teeth, one particular and prominent tooth, the completely confident intent in the eyes, the compactness, wholeness, distinctive of his intent to murder you – and you can't get out of your house, that was once your protection and the most comforting place in the world, it is now your prison, inhabited by you and the creature in the corner, who might also be slipping into other rooms, to catch you there, or there, or there – in his own good time.

SIMON 3
So I am living in a state of terror and cowardice – I am waiting to be murdered in my own house by the grinning

murderer with a knife – that is how I feel about the
tumour in my lung. Almost I want to give myself over to
him – there, there you are, do it, do it now – but mostly
I want to run and run, as if running will carry me away
from him, and not carry him along inside me, there for
the ride, enjoying it inside me, enjoying it.

SIMON 1
I went to the churchyard at the end of our street, unlocked
the gate, and walked round and around for an hour
without stopping, a very rapid plod, head lowered so I
don't have to meet the look of anyone else strolling along
the paths, keeping my eyes off any dogs with affectionate,
trouser-pawing tendencies –

SIMON 3
I felt my body surging along, even if I rightly called it
a plod, I felt a looseness in my legs, an easy swing in
my arms. I looked around to make sure there were no
witnesses.

SIMON 2
There was only a bunched-up woman with two corgi-
type dogs. She was as determined to avoid me as I was
to avoid her. I went to the top of the path and set out on
a jog. It was as if I'd never run before in my life – which
is probably why I couldn't do it – not even for three
steps, for all my legs' memory of once having sped and
flown, etc., they'd forgotten – I've forgotten – how to
run. I tried to work it out, the mechanics of it, and after
a bit of lifting my legs and pumping my arms while
stationary, I tottered forward and managed a jerky little
passage of about fifteen steps of something that was
more complicated and more urgent than a walk, but
also made me feel ill with exhaustion and shame, as if
I'd been struggling uphill with a great weight, which was

I suppose the weight of my self, accumulated over seven decades.

SIMON 3
I must get home and lie down, I thought.

SIMON 2
I headed towards the gate, which the two-corgis woman seemed to be holding open for me but wasn't, she was holding it open for her dogs.

SIMON 1
Just as I got to it she let it swing shut behind her,

SIMON 3
Clang!

SIMON 1
And hurried off with her head down, the dogs scampering playfully around her.

SIMON 2
I had to fumble for my key, locate the lock, heave it open –

SIMON 1
and here I am, having rested on the bed for a while, writing it all down and thinking as I do so

SIMON 2
that this is not the way a man should confront the fact that he's dying, how can writing of his failure to run about in the local churchyard possibly help him, and what if I'd succeeded?

SIMON 3
What if I'd sped and flown up and down the paths as once I could have done, once, once upon a time I could have done . . .

Lights close around them as they write.

SIMON 1

Scribble scribble . . .

SIMON 2

Puff puff . . .

SIMON 3

Cough cough.

Darkness.

End of Act One.

Act Two

The three Simons as at the end of Act One, except that they have exchanged positions.

SIMON 3

Scribble scribble . . .

SIMON 1

Puff puff . . .

SIMON 2

Cough cough.

SIMON 2

We all smoked when I was young, not that we were allowed to, although it's hard to see why not – given that smoking wasn't then thought to be a health hazard. It must've been a matter of decorum, a marking off of one of the stages of growing up – short trousers, long trousers, cigarettes –

SIMON 3

Our smoking was exhilaratingly furtive, the deep, dark, swirling pleasures of the smoke being sucked into fresh, pink, welcoming lungs. It took me just three or four cigarettes to acquire the habit and there are still moments when I catch more than a memory of the first suckings in, the slow leakings out when the smoke seems to fill the nostril with far more than the experience of itself,

SIMON 2

and I regret the hundreds and hundreds or thousands of cigarettes that I never experienced, inhaled and exhaled without noticing.

SIMON 1

Of course it's a truism that a cigarette is at its best after a swim,

SIMON 3

after a meal,

SIMON 2

after a fuck,

SIMON 1

and with the first cup of coffee in the morning

SIMON 3

– but their specialness is connected to the event, they are context smokes, not relished as the smokes of childhood were relished which carried with them most of all the whiff of the smoking experiences to come . . .

SIMON 1

The waiting room was large with several coffee machines and a counter where you could buy sandwiches and chocolate bars. Some of the patients had bandages around their necks with a circular hole in front, and a bit of tube that went into the throat.

SIMON 3

There was a couple, an odd, devoted couple. He a bulky and frankly rather brutish-faced man, like a biker in a film, cropped hair, tattoos, a black leather waistcoat and black leather trousers; he was very big, massive biceps and a bull neck, but quite unmenacing –

SIMON 1

I don't think it was just the circumstances that made him unmenacing – he had a soft, slightly abstracted smile and a vague, unseeing but rather tender way of looking around at the rest of us as he tended to his partner, a raddled-looking woman in a shapeless yellow dress with stringy black hair and a peaky face,

SIMON 2
and, most noticeably, a throat-bandage with a plug in it.

SIMON 3
He kept bringing her various items from the counter,
a mug of coffee and then a sandwich, which she put in
her pocket, and then a chocolate bar, and then another
chocolate bar, one of which she put in her pocket, the
other she shared with him.

SIMON 1
They each had a packet of cigarettes, Marlboro, and a
lighter each, which they kept on the arms of their chairs,
very visibly, and he took some cigarettes out of his
packet and gave them to her, she put all but one into her
own packet, and kept the one in her fingers, as if about
to smoke it seemingly quite unconscious of – of the
what? –

SIMON 2
inappropriateness, is the word, I suppose. Inappropriate
in the waiting room of a famous cancer hospital.

SIMON 3
At one point he whispered something to her and it was
hard to keep one's eyes off the cigarette between her
fingers, the black tube in her throat – I wondered if she
could speak, and whether she would actually plug the
cigarette into the plug in her throat.

SIMON 1
It didn't bear thinking about really.

SIMON 3
Nor the fact that I had a pack of Silk Cut and a lighter in
my own pocket, that didn't bear thinking about –

SIMON 2
Because I wanted a cigarette so badly, it was hurting –

SIMON 1
A nurse came and called out my name.

SIMON 3
Victoria and I stood up, side by side. Then side by side we followed the nurse down to Dr Rootle's office.

SIMON 1
My first impression, physical and before thought, was that he was a chipmunk, a massive chipmunk, and then the second one, when he'd transformed into a man, was that he was in the wrong clothes, that they were too grown-up for him. In fact, he looked like an exuberant prep school boy circa the period I went to prep school.

SIMON 3
He went behind his desk and gestured us to chairs facing him. Victoria and I sat down.

SIMON 1
He remained standing, and addressed us as follows:

SIMON 2
(*as Rootle*)
There are, as I think you know, Mr Gray, two possibilities. One, the tumour on your neck is an independent tumour, in which case it can be treated separately, either by surgery or by chemotherapy. The second possibility is that the tumour on your neck is a secondary of the tumour in your lung. That would mean the cancer cells are in your blood stream and the treatment – by radiotherapy – would be palliative: a matter of keeping the cancer in check, but not curing it. The question as to whether we are confronted by possibility one or possibility two will be answered by the operation to be performed by Mr Morgan Morgan. Now – is there anything you want to ask me?

SIMON 1

I knew what he wanted me to ask.

SIMON 3

I wasn't going to ask it.

SIMON 1

No, I don't think so.

SIMON 2

Mrs Gray?

SIMON 3

No, thank you.

SIMON 1

He sat down behind his desk and ogled us.

SIMON 3

Finally, he spoke.

SIMON 2

Well, would you like a prognosis? I mean, if the operation doesn't reveal a cancer in the throat, would you like a prognosis?

SIMON 1

It was most peculiar, most peculiar, the way he got this out, awkward, impetuous and alarmed, with a throb of excitement in it.

SIMON 3

No, certainly not. I don't want to hear that.

SIMON 1

Dr Rootle nodded at her inattentively, his ogle was fixed on me. The word 'prognosis' made me dizzy.

SIMON 3

We haven't had a definitive diagnosis yet, have we, and presumably that can't happen until after the operation.

SIMON 2

That is true, Mrs Gray.

SIMON 1

So how long after the operation, I wondered, would it take them to reach a definitive diagnosis? 'How long,' I began, then stopped. I didn't really want to prolong the conversation; it was time to go home. But Dr Rootle decided that 'How long' was the whole of the question, how long did I have to live, he took me to mean. The words came out of the side of his mouth, low but clear.

SIMON 2

About a year.

SIMON 1

I looked at Victoria, who shrank, looked small and white. I wanted to say 'But I didn't ask that question, so kindly withdraw your answer.' I wanted to swear at him – 'You stupid fucking awful fucking moron' sort of stuff.

SIMON 3

I stared at his face, now for the first time, quite calm and solemn, with a certain satisfaction in it.

SIMON 2

'Mission accomplished! Difficult deed done, and out of the side of my mouth too!'

SIMON 1

I wanted to kill him. (*He pulls out a revolver.*) A year, eh . . .? Well, that's a year longer than you've got, matey. (*Shoots Dr Rootle.*) The thing I think I understood immediately, before I'd even thought about it, was that a doctor who tells you that you have a year to live has taken that year from you – from the moment of the sentence delivered – the sentence that delivered the sentence – the knowledge would never be cleared from my consciousness, the last thought at night, the first in the morning, for the rest of my life.

SIMON 2
He said something I didn't understand about our next meeting, came around his desk and shook Victoria's hand, then held out his hand to me, and as I took it, in all its capability and power,

SIMON 3
the hand of a grown man, a true adult, he rested his other hand on my shoulder, and said, gently, almost sotto voce,

SIMON 2
'Don't worry. We'll take care of you.'

SIMON 1
Later, alone, I tried to make myself cry, as if crying would bring release, but release from what? There was nothing to be released from – I wasn't in any pain. In fact I hadn't felt so well, physically, for a long time, not for a couple of years. Knowledge, perhaps. Yes, it must've been knowledge I wanted to be released from.

SIMON 2
(an angry doctor)
You've smoked sixty cigarettes a day for the last fifty years and written boastfully about it – what did you expect? Everybody told you and warned you – indeed threatened you with exactly what's happening to you! Talk about serves you right! Talk about your own fault! And now you come to us and ask us to make you well again! How can we make a man well after fifty years of sixty a day! Well we can't– *can't*, understand? – *can't*! – simple as that! And I'm glad we can't, it'd make nonsense of cause and effect, crime and punishment, if ever a man deserved to die from lung cancer, that man is standing before me now, cap in hand – hah!

SIMON 3

Actually, it would be fag in hand, if only I had the nerve.
I've never needed cigarettes more than when getting the
news that I'm dying from them.

SIMON 1

So what can I hope for?

SIMON 3

Wisdom?

SIMON 2

I have none.

SIMON 3

Consolation?

SIMON 1

I am inconsolable. I have no faith that is – in one of the
current phrases I hate so much –

SIMON 2

'fit for purpose'.

SIMON 3

And I have no faith that isn't 'fit for purpose' either –
but do I have any sort of faith, even a small, uneasy one,
not perhaps 'fit for purpose' but a helpful guide through
the moment-by-moment moments that I have left to live
through?

SIMON 2

Of course not.

SIMON 1

I have only the self I've been stuck with all my life –

SIMON 3

odd that I should think that I am an 'I' that has a self, as
if I and my self weren't identical –

72

SIMON 1

I certainly behave as if I were in some way double, if not actually plural, especially in the last few years when I talk to myself almost continuously when on my own,

SIMON 2

and sometimes when I'm not,

SIMON 3

and also have the sense that I'm in the audience, a commentator or a judge of a debate when the dialogue becomes quarrelsome, which it frequently does –

SIMON 1

recently, since 'the news', we've spoken lamentations to ourself –

SIMON 1, 2, 3

Oh poor Simon,

SIMON 1

we say.

SIMON 1, 2, 3

Poor old Si –

SIMON 1

Affectionately, sometimes, as to a dog – or savagely sometimes more savagely, with a terrible pent-up rage.

Simon 1 suddenly attacks Simon 2.

You stupid bugger! You stupid stupid bugger bugger!

The verbal attack becomes a physical assault; they punch and wrestle each other with a desperate rage.

Stupid fucking arsehole! It's all your stupid fucking fault!

Simon 3 tries to separate them.

SIMON 3

Stop it! Stop it!

SIMON 2

Cunt! Arsehole! Stupid fucking cunt –

SIMON 1

Arsehole!

SIMON 3
(*a long scream*)

Stop it, grow up – grow up the two of me!

Bloodstained and bruised, Simon 1 and Simon 2 stop fighting. They collapse, exhausted.

I suppose I meant, specifically, 'stupid' for having smoked myself to death – but also, more generally, for being a creature that dies – thinking that the relationship between me and my mortal self was a sort of arranged marriage, the fundamental terms of which I never agreed to. Could I believe that that deceived and coerced 'I' is in fact my soul, my soul 'fastened to a dying animal / It knows not what it is' – from Yeats, but I can't remember which poem,

SIMON 1

and of course he believed in the soul almost as a physical being – 'unless soul clap its hands and sing, and louder sing / For every tatter in its mortal dress' –

SIMON 3

But no, my self isn't my soul, there's too many of it, and it's grubby and it can't sing – it's probably what I have instead of a soul, and it's not soulful, it's helpless and angry.

SIMON 2

Does this mean, then, that I never expected to die?

SIMON I

Actually, I think I'll try to come back to this question later.

SIMON 2

At some point before dawn

SIMON I

I climbed into bed

SIMON 3

and clung to my wife.

SIMON 2

Clung to my wife.

SIMON I

Although Mr Morgan Morgan had a Welsh name, he was a magnificent-looking specimen of Anglo-Saxon manhood. Mummy would have adored him – 'a bit of a lady's man, my dear, such a charmer' – he was so shy and yet so easy in his manner, and his eyes had the right amount of exhaustion in them, as if he'd just come off duty –

SIMON 2
(as Morgan Morgan)

You never know what's there until you've had a proper look. The best thing is for me to operate. Then we'll know for sure – and the sooner we know for sure, the quicker we can get on with it.

SIMON 3

Get on with what?

SIMON 2

What?

SIMON I

The 'it' – what exactly is the 'it' we'll be getting on with?

SIMON 2
Ah, well. That depends on what we find.

SIMON 1
The operation was scheduled for one-thirty p.m., no food or water for eight hours before. I had a little room at the end of a ward, a sombre little room, no doubt clean in fact but grubby in atmosphere, with a history of death, it struck me, as I stood by the bed with my overnight bag, containing pyjamas, toothbrush, books, writing pad and pens in my hand.

SIMON 3
I could see in my mind's eye the line of corpses that had lain on the bed, the grieving relatives – or no grieving relatives – just the necessary functionaries cleaning and folding up the bodies of men and women of my sort of age who'd arrived clutching their overnight bags, containing pyjamas, toothbrush, books, etc.

SIMON 1
I woke from the operation some time after midnight, with a bursting bladder. It took me several minutes to get out of bed and into the bathroom, where I discovered that my bladder wouldn't empty. I passed this information on to a nurse, who passed it onto a mortifyingly pretty doctor. She came in with a gadget I recognised as a catheter, from an operation I'd had some ten years ago. She was deft as well as pretty, she had curly black hair, an olive complexion, alert brown eyes and a mouth that would have looked even more delightful if she'd allowed it to smile.

SIMON 3
It took her about three minutes to insert my penis into the catheter, or is it technically the other way round? and I screamed only once, though at length.

SIMON I

The next morning, shortly after Victoria arrived, a shifty-looking nurse poked her head around the door and said something so incomprehensible that I know it must have been in English.

SIMON 2

Sorry, I didn't quite understand . . .

SIMON 3

Mr Morgan Morgan is doing his rounds and would like to visit you if you have no objections.

SIMON I

No objections at all. I shall be very glad to see Mr Morgan Morgan. I want to ask him about the operation.

SIMON 3

Thank you, Mr Gray, I'll tell him.

SIMON I

A few minutes later Mr Morgan Morgan appeared with the shifty little nurse-figure, who I now realised was a shifty little doctor-figure, junior doctor or trainee doctor or whatever they're called – there were eight or nine of them, young men and women who stood there all looking shifty – at least in relation to me, none of them able to meet my eye.

SIMON 2
(Morgan Morgan)

How are you feeling, Mr Gray?

SIMON I

Fine, really, under the circumstances. Sore throat, of course. But apart from that . . .

SIMON 2

Excellent. I have some good news. We did not find anything bad in your throat, except a slightly septic tonsil, which I took out. But that was all. No sign of cancer in the throat.

SIMON I
I thought the good news would be if you found cancer. (He gave me a confused smile, as if I were being too clever for him.) Your not finding cancer in my throat means that the cancer on my neck is a secondary from the cancer in my lung.

SIMON 2
Well, yes, there is that.

SIMON 3
He tried to think of something else to say.

SIMON 2
Er – well, thank you – thank you for letting us come in to see you.

SIMON I
He went out, his students trailing after him, one or two of them achieving nice, apologetic smiles –

SIMON 3
on behalf of youth and health to age and illness.

SIMON I
Victoria and I sat for a while. We didn't have much to say to each other. I thought it was odd that Morgan Morgan hadn't examined me or questioned me – apart from asking me how I felt. What exactly had he been showing his students or trainees or whatever they were?

SIMON 3
What was there to see except a seventy-year-old man in a bed on a drip? They couldn't see the catheter, and wouldn't have needed to anyway, as they surely knew what a catheter was and did. From where they stood

they couldn't have seen the tumour on my neck, so
what was it he was showing them, why did he want
them to look at me? Unless, of course, I was his straight
man in a little demonstration, or skit even, on how to
dress dreadful news up as its opposite.

SIMON 2
The next morning a nurse called Martha came to remove
my catheter. She was a rather stern-looking woman of
about forty-five, and was from Barbados. I felt uneasy
every time she came into the room as she confirmed my
sense that I was there in foul circumstances – catheter,
drip, tumours – because I deserved to be. She stood at
the end of the bed, looking at me, somehow forbidding
me to speak.

SIMON 3
Are you still writing?

SIMON 1
I beg your pardon?

SIMON 3
Writing. Are you still writing?

SIMON 1
Well, yes. Not much at the moment, of course.

SIMON 3
I write. I'm a writer too.

SIMON 1
Oh really?

SIMON 2
I wanted the person who was going to take the catheter
tube out of my penis to want something from me, and
I could sense that Martha wanted something – I couldn't
wait to promise it to her, whatever it was.

SIMON I

What have you written?

SIMON 3

A novel. I've written a novel about my adventures.

SIMON I

Have you had an adventurous life?

SIMON 3

I have, yes. A lot of strange things have happened to me since my escape from Barbados.

SIMON I

Your escape from Barbados . . .?

SIMON 3

I thought I'd call it *Dangerous Escape*, or *My Dangerous Escape*.

SIMON I

'My' is better.

SIMON 3

You think so?

SIMON I

Makes it more personal.

SIMON 3

My Dangerous Escape.

SIMON 2

She seemed to like the sound of it, and said it several times more, lengthening it slightly –

SIMON 3

My Dane–ger–ous Es–cape.

SIMON I

What were you escaping from?

SIMON 2
For me Barbados had been one of the places I escaped to, and never wanted to leave.

SIMON 3
From Barbados.

SIMON 2
Well I suppose if you were born there, with the prospect of spending the rest of your life there, you might come to feel you were on too little land in far too much water – and then there would be the family – parents, brothers and sisters, cousins, aunts, uncles – and the church – there are lots of churches of so many denominations in Barbados, that it would be hard not to belong to one of them, yes, a Godfearing people, a neighbour-fearing people, too, probably – so a perfect place for clapped-outs like me, who yearn for the England of the 1950s, but for Martha when she'd been young it might've been a prison.

SIMON 1
I suppose it's all in the book. Why you wanted to escape.

SIMON 3
That's right. That's the story.

SIMON 1
Well I must say it sounds very – very promising.

SIMON 2
I kept thinking of her fingers working the tube out of my penis, and longed to speak words that would make them gentle, coaxing, caring, loving, above all painless . . .

SIMON 3
How do you think I could get it published?

SIMON 1
Not easy. I mean – difficult. It's not easy getting a book published these days.

SIMON 2

I didn't tell her that her chances of getting *My Dangerous Escape* published were miniscule unless her story included rape, alcoholism, drug addiction, racial abuse and sexual servitude.

SIMON 1

Best thing is to get an agent.

SIMON 3

An agent?

SIMON 1

An agent will know all the publishers. She'll know which one to send your book to.

SIMON 3

You have an agent?

SIMON 1

I do, yes.

SIMON 2

She didn't say anything, just stood there, fixing me with her level authoritarian gaze.

SIMON 1

Tell you what. I've got an idea. Why don't I give you my agent's address? Perhaps she could help you. Her name is Judy Daish.

SIMON 2

I reminded myself that Judy was always at her best in a crisis, and that the removal of a catheter was a crisis. Martha took a pad out of her pocket, and a pen –

SIMON 3

Judy what? – Dash?

SIMON 1

Daish. D-A-I-S-H. Good luck with it.

Thank you.

She took the tube out in a very simple and straightforward
manner. She was very practised, but not particularly
sensitive – I mean, she didn't seem either touched or
irritated by my scream of pain. After this one conversation
she didn't refer to *My Dangerous Escape* again. The
subject was closed.

We were hanging about in the corridor, waiting for a
doctor to come and sign the document that made it OK
for me to leave, when an exceptionally pretty Indian nurse
came up to us and, with a dazzling smile to Victoria,
turned to me and said in an intimate and caring voice,
'I hope you won't mind my mentioning it, but you smell
of urine.' 'Are you sure? I can't smell anything.' 'I don't
mean to offend you. I was worried that if you go home by
bus or on the tube people might say something, and you'll
be embarrassed. Please don't mind my mentioning it.'

And she went off gracefully, on long and shapely legs,
her charming head held high. I turned to Victoria:

Do I smell of urine?

There's a uriney smell coming from somewhere. I don't
think it's you, I think it's that room there.

The door was open. Two old men lay on beds, propped
up on pillows, facing each other, asleep. They were both
sallow, gaunt and bald, so similar to each other that they
looked related, twins almost,

SIMON 3

though I don't expect they were.

SIMON 1

We've got to get away!

SIMON 3

We've got to get away!

SIMON 2

Normally we go to Greece, to Spetses – but the weather can be unreliable at this time of the year. So we thought – well,

SIMON 1 *and* 3

Crete!

SIMON 2

So here we are – in Crete – enjoying the most heavenly day – warm, with the mildest of breezes, the sea calm and the surrounding mountains visible, with the distinct hint, like large thoughts not yet thought, of mountains beyond them, and beyond. It's the sort of day that helps people to be friends, almost everyone who passes by me nods or smiles, some say a few words, the routine words – 'What a beautiful day, what a really beautiful day' . . .

SIMON 1

After lunch we decided to drive along the road towards the town, as I thought I'd glimpsed a beach or two along the way, and about halfway between the hotel and St Nikolas there was indeed a beach, a public beach, so we drove into the parking area, which was both neatly organised and commodious – none of the usual rubbish you see lying about parking areas in England, furthermore the beach was clean, even though it was crowded – people on sun-beds, sprawled on towels, horsing about with balls and frisbees. The atmosphere

84

jolly and pleasant, the sand was soft, the kind you can shake off easily once your feet are dry, and the sea was clean, shallow enough for children to play in quite a long way out, and then deep enough to have a proper swim.

SIMON 2

There was an elegant little café on stilts, where Victoria sat and read while I went off for a stroll along the promenade,

SIMON 1

past cafés and restaurants,

SIMON 2

noting that the sea got deeper and deeper,

SIMON 1

there were cement squares from which you could dive straight in and a ladder to climb down.

SIMON 2

I was thinking how delightful it all was when I suddenly began to feel hot,

SIMON 3

too hot,

SIMON 2

and a bit dizzy.

SIMON 3

I ought to get back to Victoria!

SIMON 1

But can't face the walk –

SIMON 2

Have I got the nerve to swim?

SIMON 3

Haven't got the energy, haven't got the strength, therefore haven't got the nerve,

SIMON 2

then I thought, well, what the hell,

SIMON 1

what the hell,

SIMON 2

went to some nearby steps, and climbed down into the
sea –

SIMON 3

cool,

SIMON 2

cool and refreshing –

SIMON 1

I took it very slowly, very gently, on my side, leisurely
strokes on my side, thinking I could always turn back
to the ladder,

SIMON 3

but suddenly it was too late,

SIMON 2

I was as far from the ladder as from the beach.

SIMON 1

Nothing for it but to toil on,

SIMON 3

to assume a calm and easy air, turning my arm over
languidly, as if really I were idling along on my side,

SIMON 2

but my stroke was getting feebler,

SIMON 1

my legs kept dropping under me, to the vertical,

SIMON 2

getting them up again was becoming a conscious and
laborious act,

SIMON 3

but still I was all right, making sure that my breathing was steady and regular,

SIMON 2

strolling, strolling along in the water, not panicking.

SIMON 1

I rolled on my back, and looked up at the sky, letting my body drift,

SIMON 2

drift,

SIMON 3

sort of knowing I was drifting,

SIMON 2

drifting away from shore,

SIMON 3

out to sea,

SIMON 1

there was a slight tightening in one of my calves, from cramp, and so the first stirrings of real panic.

SIMON 3

I let myself hang loosely, so that I was a-tilt, my head above water, my body trailing out under it but comfortable,

SIMON 2

floating,

SIMON 3

drifting.

SIMON 1

The pain eased in my calf,

87

SIMON 3

and I had that feeling I have sometimes in the sea, of
wanting to go on drifting, and on,

SIMON 2

until I drift far away,

SIMON 3

finally drifting under water without noticing a change,

SIMON 2

simply a slipping out of two elements into one,

SIMON 1

seeping into the sea,

SIMON 3

scarcely a death, really,

SIMON 2

so much better than rotting in bed,

SIMON 1

so very much better . . .

SIMON 3

but I can't!

SIMON 2

Impossible, I can't!

SIMON 1

I can't leave Victoria reading in the café,

SIMON 3

alone in Crete,

SIMON 2

having to arrange to take my body back if it washed
ashore,

SIMON 1

waiting weeks for me to turn up,

SIMON 2

wrapped in seaweed,

SIMON 3

what was left of me, after the fish had had their fill.

SIMON 1

The thoughts rolled as I lay tilted upwards in the water, with the sun beating down on my head, and without planning it I began to haul myself back towards shore,

SIMON 2

towards the beach,

SIMON 1

arm over, arm over, arm over, la la la, la la –

SIMON 3

Soon I was amongst people again, first of all the grown-ups in singles or in pairs, then mothers and fathers playing with their children and teaching them to swim, or dunking the babies, and then I was on the beach – almost the most difficult part, getting to my feet and wading to the shore.

SIMON 1

I plodded across the hot sand, around recumbent young couples who were holding hands with their faces turned towards each other, went into one of the dressing rooms, sat on the bench in a collapse, went really into a sort of coma for a while.

SIMON 3

Then it occurred to me that I'd been gone quite a long time, Victoria might have begun to worry.

SIMON 1

As I picked my way across the sand, I was actually rather proud of myself. I climbed the steps to the café, and saw Victoria standing up at the table, the book in her hand, staring anxiously along the promenade. I wanted to boast – 'I've walked and then I swam, for oh miles and miles' – though I hadn't, more like a half a mile each way, well, perhaps half a mile altogether. Anyway I didn't say anything other than 'I'm back.'

SIMON 2
I'm back.

SIMON 3
Where have you been?

SIMON 2
Oh, walked along the path a bit, went in for a dip –

SIMON 1
I picked up a towel and went off to shower and change, and then we had lunch there: Victoria a health-giving salad, and I multiple layers of bread with nothing identifiable between them, but it was pleasant, shady and peaceful, lots to look at on the beach, and no music – no music, so who cared what was in the sandwich?

SIMON 3
As soon as we got back to London I went to see Harold. I took with me a book I'd intended to give him on his birthday. He's been in hospital again. He came out a couple of days ago but is still, Antonia said, very weak, couldn't go out but would welcome a visit, she thought.

SIMON 2
He was in his usual armchair, with a fire blazing in the grate, its flames orange and blue. I gave him the book, then sat in the armchair opposite him, on the other side of the fire. He looked into the book, Keith Miller's autobiography, written over fifty years ago, which I bought secondhand over forty years ago and is long out of print. I thought Harold would like it and be touched

by the photographs, the sort you don't see any more,
grey and white and one-dimensional, the men with
Brylcreemed hair and smiling, shiny faces, and the clothes,
of course – the cricketers either in long-sleeved white
shirts and creased white flannels belted tightly at the
waist, or in drab grey suits with fedoras and trilbys.
The prose is cheerful and kindly, lots of anecdotes but
no gossip, nothing revealed but the spirit of the age and
the modest decency of the writer, who was, in fact, also
a gambler and a womaniser, one of Princess Margaret's
lovers and a bit of a home-wrecker and so forth as well
as a war hero – an incomparable man, really.

SIMON 3

Harold dipped into a few places, smiled and grunted, put
the book down and we looked at each other. So there
we were, two elderly and ailing men who'd known each
other for half our lifetimes.

SIMON 1

We talked bitterly about the things that were most on
our minds – sickness, hospitals, colonoscopies, catheters,
the sheer helplessness and humiliation of it all. His voice
got stronger the longer we talked, and we both got more
cheerful, the absurdity of it, that such things could be
happening to us, who in so many important respects
hadn't yet reached our maturity, we still had miles to go
before we slept, miles to go.

SIMON 3

After we'd been at it for about an hour or so I thought
he must be getting tired, I was feeling a little tired myself
and was on the point of getting up when he reached for
the book –

SIMON 2

Thanks for this.

He opened it, looked closely at one of the photographs,
and remarked that there was going to be the annual
meeting of his cricket club, the Gaieties, in a few days
time, he wouldn't be able to go himself, he said, wouldn't
be up to it, but they'd asked him if he'd do a little speech
on video, and he'd decided that this was what he was
going to tell them: that in one of his first matches as
captain, forty odd years ago, the opposing side's best
batsman was in, and going ominously well until he skied
a catch, very high, with Harold directly under it – he
mimed himself gazing anxiously upwards, then jerking
from side to side to get into the right position, then
cupping his hands, then watching the ball as it fell
through his hands and dropped at his feet. The next ball
the batsman repeated the shot, the ball went up, came
down through Harold's hands to land once again at his
feet. The batsman went on to make a hundred. When it
came to the Gaieties turn to bat their best batsman was
going well, with a big score and possibly victory in sight,
when a wicket fell and Harold came out to join him.
In no time Harold had run him out. A few balls later
Harold was bowled neck and crop. The Gaieties lost by an
enormous margin, entirely because of Harold's versatile
performance. He told the story with such vigour and relish
it was as if we were suddenly, thirty-five years ago, both
back having a boozy lunch in our favourite restaurant,
L'Epicure in Romilly Street, a week before rehearsals. At
its conclusion we both laughed and laughed until we both
coughed and coughed,

SIMON 2

laughed and coughed,

SIMON 1

coughed and laughed.

SIMON 3

Dr Rootle led us into his office, where we sat on two
hard-backed chairs facing his desk, and he sat behind it,
looking down at a folder,

SIMON 2

my folder I assumed,

SIMON 3

then took out what looked like an X-ray,

SIMON 2

my scan I assumed.

SIMON 3

He put the scan back into the folder and smiled,

SIMON 2

a huge smile as he has huge teeth, huge and white,

SIMON 3

that could make you feel like Little Red Riding Hood.

SIMON 2

What followed was very confusing, and I can't recall,
though I've tried, the exact words – in fact I have an idea
that I didn't understand them, nor did Victoria,

SIMON 3

and we looked at one another for help.

SIMON 1

Part of the problem was Dr Rootle's manner: it seemed
playful, almost teasing,

SIMON 2

his eyes sparkled and bulged behind his spectacles,

SIMON 3

and his teeth continued to flash –

he looked more than ever like a large schoolboy – and then we realized,

SIMON 1, 2, 3

almost simultaneously,

SIMON 3

he thought we knew the results of the scan! And I said –

SIMON 1

No, no, that's why we're here,

SIMON 3

to be told the results.

SIMON 1

He looked surprised, slightly disbelieving,

SIMON 3

but then our own surprise must have persuaded him that we weren't teasing him back.

SIMON 1

He didn't stop smiling as he explained that the scan showed that the radiotherapy had shrunk both tumours, and then he said:

SIMON 2
(as Rootle)

Furthermore there are no signs that the cancer has spread – although there's no question but that the cancer's still there, in the blood, and will eventually return. Now there are two ways of dealing with someone in your situation: the American way, which is to press on immediately with aggressive treatment, probably an intensive course of chemotherapy, which might prolong your life but perhaps by no more than a month or so, and would be very uncomfortable, if not downright miserable; the second way is the way we favour in this

hospital, the English way, so to speak, which is to
encourage the patient to lead as full a life as possible for
as long as possible, and not to resort to intensive
chemotherapy until it's absolutely necessary – at the end,
in other words, which in your case might be as far away
as eighteen months or even two years. What do you
think?

SIMON 3

What I thought was that Dr Rootle was the most
delightful man I'd ever met.

SIMON 2

I adored him, but I didn't say so.

SIMON 1

I said instead that it was better news than I'd dared
hope.

SIMON 2

I stood up and held out my hand. He shook it, then
shook Victoria's hand, and came around the desk to
open the door for us.

SIMON 1

I noticed that he didn't put his hand on my shoulder or
clasp and squeeze my elbow,

SIMON 2

which I took to be a confirmation that I was out of the
compassion zone for eighteen months or even two – two
years! Two whole years!

SIMON 3

I went there this afternoon. Piers's little section was *en
fête*, quite extraordinary, not simply the abundance of
flowers on every grave, including Piers's, but flags, bunting,
balloons, dolls, as if transformed into the setting for a
party, a victory party. Where was the music, one wondered,
and where the voices? – because it was as quiet as it

usually is, with just the sound of a car or a mower in the distance, and it was as sunny as it usually is – there's always bright sunshine when I visit Piers, not at all a coincidence or a mystical harmony between me and the weather, it's simply that I never go there unless the sun is out, partly to make sure that I associate his grave with cheerfulness and brightness, though not entirely with warmth, as my favourite time is on a cold, bright winter midday, and partly because I never want to go unless the sun is out, in fact the impulse only comes with the sun, and I can see myself now, as I write this – yes, there I am, an elderly man, sitting on the bench in the sunshine. I have half a newspaper on my lap. The other half – the business, travel and property sections – is under my buttocks, to cushion them against the wood of the bench. I imagine that the few people who pass by, usually in clusters of three or so, would take me for what I am, a brother visiting a younger brother, rather than a husband grieving for a wife, or a father for a lost child. I don't know what precisely would make this evident, it wouldn't really be anything in the detail, more a general effect, but one can always distinguish the brothers from the husbands and the fathers, at least I can, I think, and I therefore assume others can as well, but we might all of us be wrong. I might be identified, for instance, as one of those creatures who likes to visit graveyards, I was going to say 'strange creatures' but when I think about it I see nothing strange in it, there are few more interesting places in London than Kensal Green Cemetery, and few more enchanted and eloquent spots than Rowan Gardens, or more vivacious, at least on an afternoon when the bunting and the flags are out, and balloons floating, and there is the sense of victory in the air, not grim and forceful victory, as in 'Death, be not proud' – but a jolly victory, a celebration as of a – what? I can't think what sort of event would be collectively celebrated in Rowan Gardens in a manner that made it look like a village fair from a different age – how come the balloons and flags? and who put the flowers on Piers's grave? There were two bunches, a bunch of fresh daffodils and a bunch, a clutch, really, of artificial poppies, they must have been laid by different hands – now, as I sit here writing this, I realise that none of it makes sense – if it was in memory of a momentous event, a great battle won or a country liberated, they would leave a sign, surely – it begins now to feel like a hallucination, the question being whether I had the hallucination when I visited Piers this afternoon or am having it now, in memory, in memory decorating with flags, bunting and balloons that sedate and pleasant place I know so well.

SIMON 1

Two years!

SIMON 2

I mean two years . . .

SIMON 1

two whole –

SIMON 3

well, eighteen months –

SIMON 2

yes, let's keep it at eighteen months –

SIMON 1

eighteen months, to avoid disappointment.

The Simons stand smiling at each other as the lights fade.

The End.